WHAT WAS DAILY LIVING LIKE IN A TYPICAL GREEK TOWN?

HISTORY BOOKS FOR KIDS

Children's History Books

In this book, we're going to talk about daily life in a typical town in Ancient Greece. So, let's get right to it!

Deep Blue of the Aegean Sea, Greek Islands, Greece.

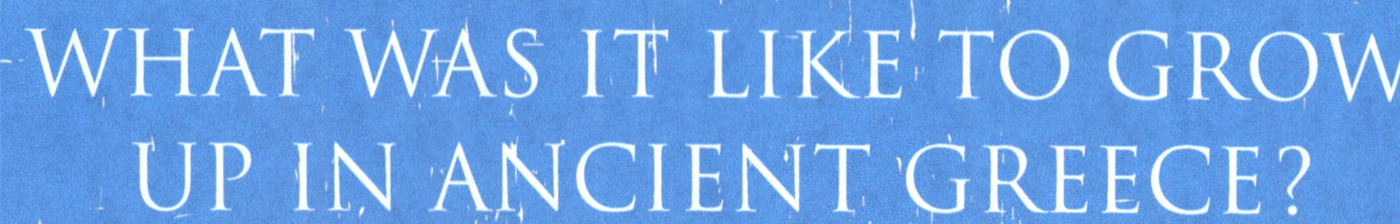

The father in a household could decide whether a new baby would be raised by their family or not. If the baby was a girl, or was weak or diseased, the father could choose not to take the child. Once the father made a decision that the child was going to be raised by their family, the child was nurtured and cared for. The children in a household would have toys to share and games to play.

Traditional greek village, Zakynthos,
Ionian islands, Greece.

At the age of seven, boys began their formal education. At school, the boys studied math, writing, and reading. If they showed musical talent, they would be taught to play an instrument. As boys got older, they were also taught debate and logic skills. Girls weren't allowed to attend school. They were taught domestic skills at home. In Ancient Greece girls didn't have the opportunities that modern girls have today.

WHAT WERE ANCIENT GREEK HOMES LIKE?

Ancient Greek homes were designed so that the people who lived there wouldn't get too hot in the summer or too cold in the winter. They were made of mud bricks that had been dried in the sun and solidified. There were some small windows with no glass, but unlike most modern houses today, the windows were constructed high on the walls.

View of old town in Chania, Crete.

They weren't designed for people to look out, only to let light in. When the sun was too hot, the windows were covered with wood shutters. The roofs were constructed with tiles made of clay.

Most Greek houses weren't very large, although upper middle class and wealthy families had larger homes. Those who were wealthy had artwork created for their inside walls and colorful mosaic tiles for flooring.

Pictorial streets of old Greece (Chania - Crete)

THE COURTYARD

The outdoor roofless courtyard was the core of activity of the home. The courtyard offered a fun area to play, a place to fetch water from the well, and a place to make an offering to the gods and goddesses, especially to Hestia who was the goddess of the hearth. The other rooms of the house were organized around this central courtyard. On hot days, the women of the house might do some weaving or spinning while they were seated outdoors.

Greek Courtyard

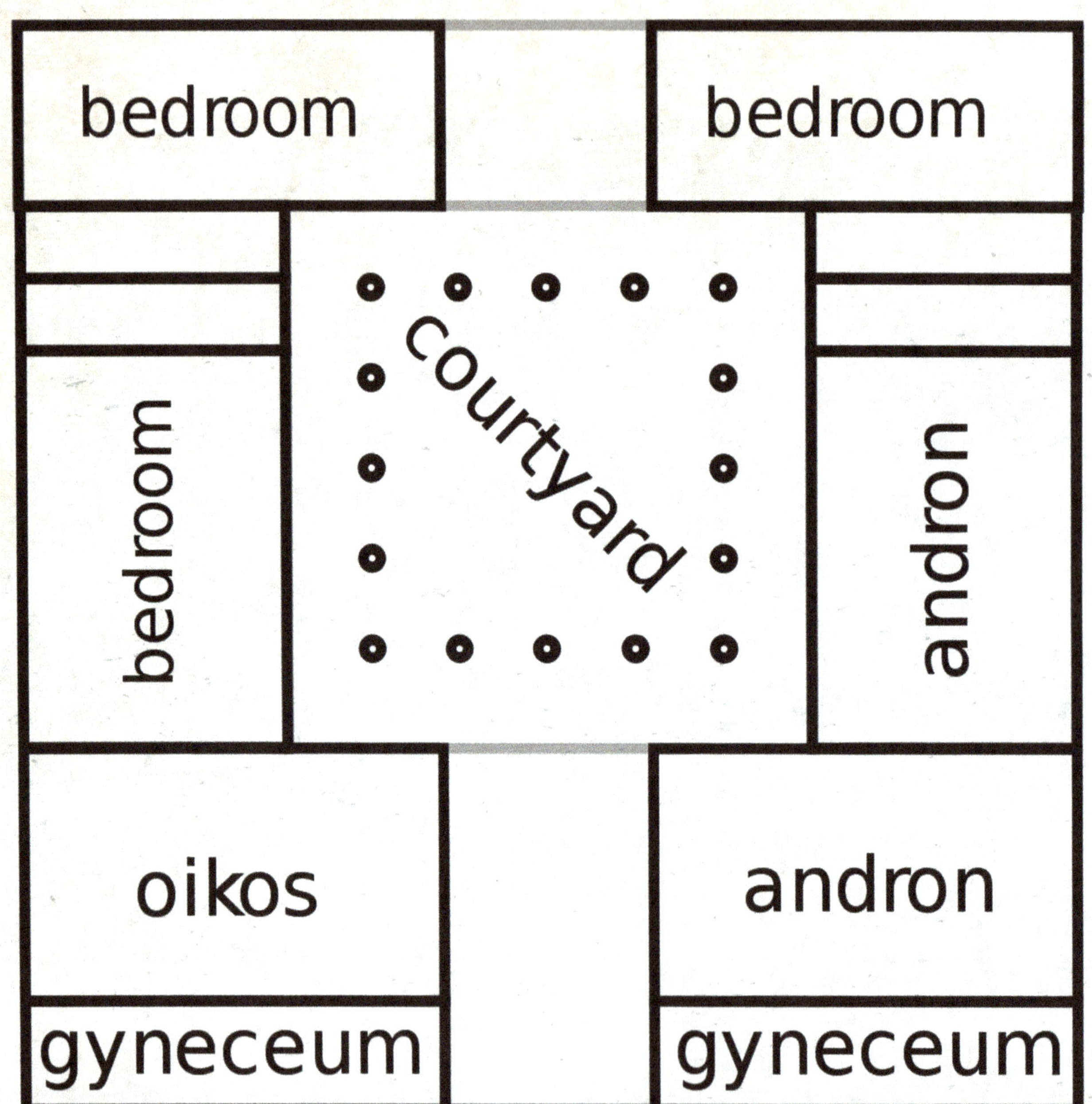

Greek House Layout

THE ANDRON

The men had separate living areas than the women. One of the reasons that women had a separate dwelling area was so they would not be seen by any male guests who were visiting the house. The man of the house would have an Andron or Androntis, which was a special room that might be called a *"man cave"* today. Men used this area of the house to drink, eat, and socialize with their men friends and business colleagues.

They had special social get-togethers that they called **Symposia.** This room had the most elaborate furniture in the house.

The ladies of the house were not allowed in this room, but both male and female slaves attended to the guests and sometimes women entertainers danced for the men.

A symposium (pl: symposia) was a drinking party in Ancient Greece. Guests were males. Well bred women did not attend.

THE GYNAIKON

There was also a special room in the house where women could socialize. It was upstairs as far away as possible from the sometimes noisy presence of men in the Andron. In this special room, called a Gynaikon or Gynaikonitis, they socialized with their women family members and friends. They sat together as they sewed, chatted, and played with the children.

Pebble floor mosaic depicting Bellerophon scene in a house in the ancient city of Olynthos, Chalkidiki, Greece.

THE STOREROOM

Downstairs there was a storeroom for large jars that held grain for grinding into flour as well as freshly picked olives. Wine was stored there as well. Usually there was a separate area set aside as a workroom for the slaves to design and make jewelry or to weave sandals.

Old traditional storage inside a Greek monastery.

THE KITCHEN

There was a central fire hearth for cooking in the kitchen area. The fire created a lot of smoke so there was a hole constructed in the roof so the smoke would go out of the house. Large, rustic clay cooking pots were used to prepare most of the everyday meals. There were also decorative pots and plates, but these were only used for special occasions.

Metal antique Greek tableware.

 any of these kitchen items have been discovered on archaeological digs and the elaborate designs on them have provided lots of information about daily life in Ancient Greece.

Old traditional kitchen inside a Greek monastery at Meteora.

THE BEDROOMS AND BATHROOM

The bedrooms in the house were very simple. The beds were like basic couches. Plain wooden chests stored the needed bedding and clothes. The Ancient Greeks didn't have indoor plumbing, but they did usually have bathtubs for soaking and chamber pots to use as toilets.

Bey Hamam (turkish baths), Thessaloniki, Greece.

WHAT FOOD DID THEY EAT?

The Ancient Greeks ate a diet that would be called a Mediterranean diet today. They ate vegetables and fruit. They also enjoyed freshly caught fish and olives, which were a staple in their diet. Wine mixed with water and different types of cheeses would be served daily as well. Meat, such as pork or cuts of beef, were only eaten during festivals or special occasions.

Dolma, a Greek traditional appetizer.

They might have a hunk of bread dipped in olive oil for breakfast and different variations of cooked fish, grains, and vegetables during the day. They didn't eat sugar, so if they had anything sweet it was made with natural honey.

Ancient Greek female clothing.

WHAT TYPES OF CLOTHES DID THEY WEAR?

The clothes that the Ancient Greeks wore were made of a wool material that was thin. They made this material into tunics called **Chitons.** Both men and women wore these tunics. They were made from a large piece of rectangular cloth that was cut in two pieces.

Women's Clothing - Greek (left) and Roman (right)

GREEK. 10. ANCIENT TIMES.

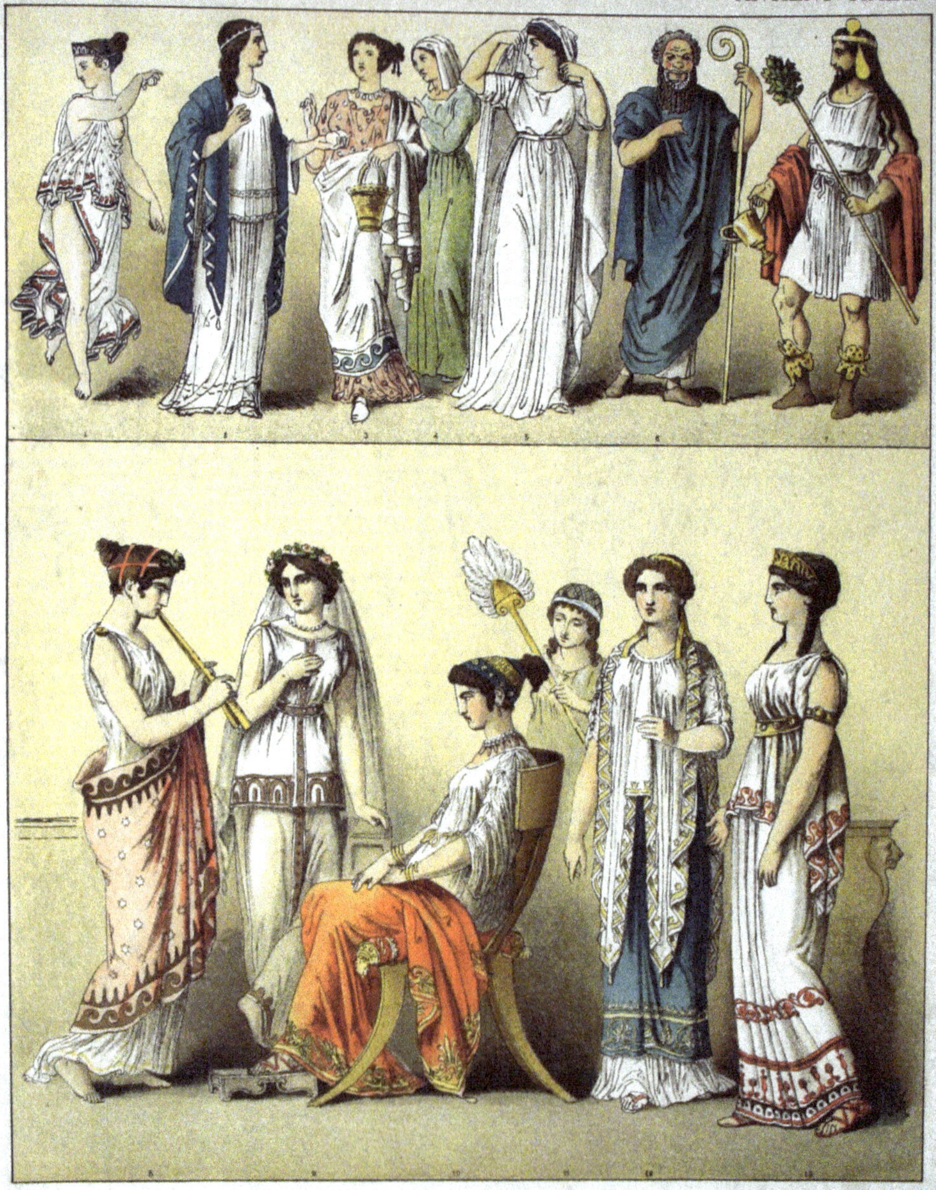

1. Female Dancer. 2.-5. Women. 6. 7. Actors. 8. Female Flute-player. 9.-13. Women.

To keep the tunic on, it had fasteners at different points on the body, and a belt to tie it in at the waist. The garments came in different colors and lengths for variations. The wealthy could afford linen fabric or silk for their Chitons.

WHAT TYPES OF JOBS DID THEY HAVE?

Women in Greece were almost always homemakers. They raised the children, prepared the meals, took care of the clothing, and tended to the home and hearth.

Men had many different types of jobs. The men could be farmers or fishermen. Farmers and fishermen traded their goods at the marketplace so they could feed their own families.

Old view of Corfu island, Ionian sea.

Many men were soldiers who battled to gain territory for Greece or to defend the country from enemies. Others were merchants, teachers, or craftsmen. Some skilled craftsmen were more like artists. They created beautiful sculptures and paintings or mosaics made of tiny tiles.

Other artists made pottery with detailed decorations, jewelry, and metal coins. In some cities, the houses were organized by occupation, so the farmers would live in one area and the soldiers in another.

AIONYS

There was also a wealthy, elite group of Greeks who didn't need to labor as much as the middle and lower classes. They could afford the luxury of sending their children to special schools, such as Plato's Academy. There, students could learn about philosophy and logical reasoning. There were also specialized schools for those with art talent so they could learn painting, architecture, or sculpture.

Most of the cities and towns in Ancient Greece were organized by a region called a city-state. City-states had their own governments. The government was usually housed at the city's center, which was close to the acropolis. The acropolis was usually a hill or mountainside where a temple and other religious shrines were located.

The North Theatre in ancient Jerash, was most likely used for government meetings rather than artistic performances.

In the city center, there was also a marketplace for the public called an agora. At that location, people could shop in an open-air market, conduct business, or just meet friends and neighbors to socialize and talk. It was something like an elaborate farmer's market.

Free Greeks, both men and women, were citizens and could enjoy the privileges their government had to offer, such as protection from the violent acts of others. Their government used an early form of democracy. One major difference between the United States today and Ancient Greece is that we no longer have slaves.

Marble statues of the Great Ancient Greek scholars Socrates and Plato.

In Ancient Greece most families had slaves. The slaves couldn't vote or own property. They couldn't be elected to government positions. Their owners were in complete control of their lives.

The Greeks loved art, good music, and fine literature. They were also very social and loved sporting events, like the Olympics, which they held every four years. When the weather allowed it, they enjoyed plays and festivals outdoors. They worshipped in their temples and went shopping in their marketplaces.

Athens, Greece: The Lillehammer 2016 Winter Youth Olympic Games flame.

Ancient stone greek house.

Visit
BABY PROFESSOR
EDUCATION KIDS
www.BabyProfessorBooks.com
to download Free Baby Professor eBooks
and view our catalog of new and exciting
Children's Books